This book is dedicated to the millions of people who are part of the It's a Southern Thing community online. Thanks to y'all, we learn new Southernisms every day.

By It's a Southern Thing

Discovered, compiled and edited by:
Kelly Kazek, Haley Laurence, Amber Sutton and Jared Boyd

Illustrated by Laura Levie
Calligraphy by Amy Cash
Foreword by Sean Dietrich

Visit us at **southernthing.com**

Printed in Canada
First edition September 2019
ISBN 978-1-57571-005-1 (hardback)

FOREWORD...

Sean Dietrich is a columnist and novelist known for his commentary on life in the American South. He lives on the Florida Panhandle, where he's a mediocre sailor and fisherman, biscuit connoisseur and barbecue competition judge.

In the American South, words are sacred. Big words, small words, written words, spoken words and in some cases, swear words. Many of our words and phrases are unique to our region and would not make sense to someone living in, say, Toledo, Ohio.

For example: ***"Well, I Suwannee,"*** which when literally translated means "Well, swat my hind with a melon rind." If you were to say this in Toledo, people would look at you like you had cockroaches crawling from your ears.

We are wordy people. We cannot visit a grocery store without having conversations in every aisle. We love people and we love talking. And more than anything we love talking about people.

If you don't believe this, attend a baby shower. Chances are, ladies at the shower won't even get around to celebrating the actual baby. Not until they have discussed the personal lives of everyone living within the radius of three ZIP codes.

You want Southernisms and dialectal humor? Visit the Women's Methodist Bible Study at Debbie McDonnel's house on Wednesday night. You will hear so many old-time expressions flying around that you'll need to wear a helmet.

My mother took me to Miss Debbie's once. It was a time of serious Biblical education, by which I mean that every woman was required to bring a congealed salad. And I wish you could have been there. Those women use Southern language in its undiluted form.

They say words like: ***"reckon"*** (pronounced: reggin), and ***"Lord have mercy"*** (pronounced: Lowered a'mercy), and ***"precious"*** (pronounced: shut UP that's so CUTE!).

Southern males also have their own list of words and epigrams. Men in this part of the world use a collection of specialized highly grunts, along with occasional bodily noises to express emotion. We have grunts for a wide range of feelings. There are grunts for approval, disapproval, satisfaction, hunger, grief, physical pain, traffic violations, certain brands of spinning lures and moments of spiritual reflection.

For example: I remember the way my uncle would grunt during Baptist sermons. Whenever our preacher said something particularly good, my uncle gave a quiet grunt.

Then he'd turn to me and whisper, "If that don't light your fire, your wood's wet."

God, I love that phrase.

Likewise, if the preacher was boring one Sunday, my uncle would say in a loud and audible voice, "This guy sucks pond water." Whereupon my aunt would stab him in the chest with an emery board.

My uncle always had a way with words. But in our culture, everyone's uncle has a way with words. So does everyone's aunt, granny, granddaddy, cousin, second cousin, third cousin and insurance salesman.

Once I was in Newark, New Jersey on business. I was walking through a drugstore. I noticed an elderly man in the checkout line. He was buying a bottle of cough syrup.

The old man was obviously sick because he was coughing and sneezing. He paid for his purchase, took his plastic bag, and left the store without saying a single word to the cashier. Not even a thank you or smile. It struck me as bizarre.

This would never happen below the Mason-Dixon line. If the identical scenario took place in—I'm just spitballing here—Enterprise, Alabama, it would go something like this:

The cashier would see the man walk into the drugstore and she'd remark, "*Lowered a'mercy, Bobby, you look pitiful, what's wrong?*"

"*Oh,*" Bobby would say. "*I got the grip, everyone in my house came down with the grip this week.*"

"Well, you look about as sick as sin at the Holiday Inn."

"If I was any sicker, they'd have to kill me twice just to make me feel better."

"Bless your pea-pickin' heart, that's awful."

"Ain't it just."

"Well, I Suwannee."

And so on.

We can see from the above conversation that the cashier and Bobby have just conducted an entire conversation without saying anything important. And chances are Bobby will receive a special delivery of chicken soup with oyster crackers on his porch later that evening. Also some potato salad, and possibly a glazed ham.

Harvard English majors call these conversational tidbits "colloquialisms." But those of us who went to community college call them "stuff Granny used to say."

Take, for instance, the above phrase, ***"Well, I Suwannee."*** Perhaps your granny said this in moments of extreme consternation. But have you ever wondered why she said this? Probably because the word consternation hadn't even been invented yet. And even if it had, Granny wouldn't have known this word because Emily Post sure as hell never used it.

So our ancestors found colorful ways of expressing themselves without resorting to vulgar talk, Harvard words or swearing. And I love this about us. The color of our language is our most identifiable trait.

Experts tell us that language was important to our prehistoric ancestors because it gave them the sense of community they needed for survival, so that when invaders from the North would attack their villages, hordes of our ancestors would gather together and instinctively do the wave and shout, "Dee-fense!" Or in some remote regions, "Go for two!"

Most language historians believe that at some point during the Paleolithic Period, everyone's cave-grannies got together for an important meeting in someone's cave-living-room and invented what would become the building blocks of Southern language. Through carbon-dating techniques, scholars now know that these cavewomen served crustless cucumber finger sandwiches on Blue Danube print china for this luncheon.

Then, after washing dishes, our forebearers probably came up with a list of phrases and expressions designed to make us laugh, keep us entertained or to warn our children that their hindparts were in severe danger if they did not stop poking their sister in the backseat.

Our ancestors gave us words. Their words became our words. Many of these words and phrases we still use today. Some of them are real doozies, too. In fact, doozy is one of their words.

Here are some other phrases:

- ***It's hotter outside than a deacon jumping rope in the attic.***
- ***You're five kinds of crazy split thirteen different ways.***
- ***Used-a-could.***
- ***I'm gonna cloud up and rain all over you if you don't quit poking your sister in the backseat.***

Thusly, the purpose of this foreword is not only because I love Southern language, but because I am getting paid actual money to write this. Also, I need the money because I am so poor that for supper, I often go to KFC just to lick other people's fingers.

Which is a clear example of why it is so important to preserve regional language, or else future generations will not even know what KFC is, nor why I would go there to engage in the act of licking the fingers of complete strangers.

What I am saying is, the world is changing, and every day we lose more of it. The internet has forever altered things. The old ways are dying, and so are the white-haired people who gave them to us.

And I for one do not want to live in a world that bears no trace of those who came before me. I do not want to lose our wives' tales, folkways, dialect or small talk in the grocery store. I do not want to lose old women who still say, ***"Well, I Suwanee."***

The phrases, sayings and colloquialisms found within this collection are not only intended to entertain, but to keep our ancestors alive so that we will never forget them.

To put it in their own words: If this book don't light your fire, your wood is wet.

The South's weather is unpredictable, so you may need all these phrases in one day...

It's hotter'n the devil's armpits.

FOR THOSE EVEN HOTTER DAYS WHEN LEAVING THE HOUSE JUST ISN'T AN OPTION

IT'S AS HOT AS THE hinges ON THE gates OF hades.

FOR THOSE EVEN HOTTER DAYS WHEN LEAVING THE HOUSE JUST ISN'T AN OPTION

IT MUST BE

100

degrees

IN THE

shade.

FOR THOSE EVEN HOTTER DAYS WHEN LEAVING THE HOUSE JUST ISN'T AN OPTION

IT'S HOTTER'N *Satan's house cat.*

FOR THOSE EVEN HOTTER DAYS WHEN LEAVING THE HOUSE JUST ISN'T AN OPTION

IT'S SO DRY THE trees ARE bribing THE dogs.

WHEN YOU'RE CONVINCED THE SOUTH HAS TURNED INTO A DESERT

IT'S NOT THE
HEAT,
it's the
humidity.

FOR THOSE HUMID, HOT DAYS IN THE SOUTH *(aka every day)*

It's hotter than blue blazes.

FOR THOSE HUMID, HOT DAYS IN THE SOUTH *(aka every day)*

IT'S SO HOT
I'm sweatin'
LIKE A
pig.

FOR THOSE HUMID, HOT DAYS IN THE SOUTH *(aka every day)*

I'M

burning

slap

up.

FOR THOSE HUMID, HOT DAYS IN THE SOUTH *(aka every day)*

It's hog-killing weather.

For those days you may have to stock up on milk and bread

IT'S COLD as a wedge.

FOR THOSE DAYS YOU MAY HAVE TO STOCK UP ON MILK AND BREAD

IT'S GONNA BE

WHEN IT STARTS RAINING, NORMALLY IN THE MIDDLE OF ERRANDS

IT'S coming UP A storm.

WHEN IT STARTS RAINING, NORMALLY IN THE MIDDLE OF ERRANDS

It's blowin' up a storm.

WHEN IT STARTS RAINING, NORMALLY IN THE MIDDLE OF ERRANDS

FOR THOSE TWO DAYS OF AUTUMN

Expressions you'll need to survive Southern parenthood (besides 'hush!')

This is worse than trying to herd cats.

WHEN YOU'RE TRYING TO GET EVERYONE READY FOR CHURCH

IT WENT TO

hell

IN A

handbasket.

WELL

butter my butt

AND

call me

a biscuit.

WHEN THE KIDS ACTUALLY CLEAN THEIR ROOM AND GO TO BED ON TIME

This ain't my first rodeo.

WHEN YOU WANT TO REMIND EVERYONE WHO'S IN CHARGE

I was born at night
BUT NOT
LAST NIGHT.

WHEN YOU WANT TO REMIND EVERYONE WHO'S IN CHARGE

I'M ABOUT TO

jerk a knot in your tail.

I'M GONNA *tan* YOUR *hide.*

WHEN YOU NEED TO USE THE ULTIMATE SOUTHERN MOM-ISMS

can't
NEVER
could.

Ain't NO LESSON in the SECOND KICK of a MULE.

If it'd been a SNAKE it would've BIT YOU.

FOR THOSE MOMENTS THE KIDS (OR YOUR SPOUSE, REALLY) CAN'T FIND SOMETHING RIGHT IN FRONT OF THEM

JUST hanging on
LIKE A hair IN A
biscuit.

BUT REALLY, EVERY PARENT IS

The ways we Southerners act (besides not right)

HOW YOU REACT WHEN SOMEONE SAYS MAC AND CHEESE ISN'T A VEGGIE

SHE
PITCHED
A
hissy fit.

HOW YOU REACT WHEN SOMEONE SAYS MAC AND CHEESE ISN'T A VEGGIE

He had a conniption.

HOW YOU REACT WHEN SOMEONE SAYS MAC AND CHEESE ISN'T A VEGGIE

THEY'RE HAVING A come-to-Jesus MEETING.

I had a half mind to.

HOW YOU REACT WHEN SOMEONE SAYS MAC AND CHEESE ISN'T A VEGGIE

SHE'S AS
nervous
AS A
cat IN A room
full OF
rocking chairs.

WHEN THE PREACHER IS LONG-WINDED AND YOU DON'T THINK YOU'LL GET OUT BEFORE THE SUNDAY LUNCH RUSH

HE'S grinnin' LIKE A possum EATIN' A sweet tater.

WHAT TO SAY WHEN YOUR FAVORITE FOOTBALL TEAM WINS ON SATURDAY

WHAT TO SAY WHEN YOUR FAVORITE FOOTBALL TEAM WINS ON SATURDAY

I'M JUST AS

happy

AS A

tick ON A

fat dog:

WHAT TO SAY WHEN YOUR FAVORITE FOOTBALL TEAM WINS ON SATURDAY

She's AS happy AS A pig EATIN' SLOP.

OR, EVEN BETTER, WHEN MULTIPLE PEOPLE BRING SLOW COOKER CHEESE DIP TO THE TAILGATE

I'M FINER THAN A *frog hair split four ways.*

OR, EVEN BETTER, WHEN MULTIPLE PEOPLE BRING SLOW COOKER CHEESE DIP TO THE TAILGATE

I'M AS

happy

AS A

hog IN mud.

OR, EVEN BETTER, WHEN MULTIPLE PEOPLE BRING SLOW COOKER CHEESE DIP TO THE TAILGATE

GIMME SOME *sugar.*

WHAT GRANNY WILL TELL YOU AS SHE MAKES YOU TAKE HOME LEFTOVERS IN A COOL WHIP CONTAINER

I love you
a bushel
& a peck.

WHAT GRANNY WILL TELL YOU AS SHE MAKES YOU TAKE HOME LEFTOVERS IN A COOL WHIP CONTAINER

WELL, I swan.

WHAT GRANNY WILL TELL YOU AS SHE MAKES YOU TAKE HOME LEFTOVERS IN A COOL WHIP CONTAINER

YOU'RE JUST

pretty

AS A

picture.

WHAT GRANNY WILL TELL YOU AS SHE MAKES YOU TAKE HOME LEFTOVERS IN A COOL WHIP CONTAINER

There's no art in the world quite like a Southern insult

FOR THOSE TIMES SOMEONE REALLY NEEDS AN ATTITUDE ADJUSTMENT

HE THINKS THE
sun comes up
JUST TO
hear him
crow.

FOR THOSE TIMES SOMEONE REALLY NEEDS AN ATTITUDE ADJUSTMENT

HE'S GETTING A LITTLE *too big* FOR HIS *britches.*

FOR THOSE TIMES SOMEONE REALLY NEEDS AN ATTITUDE ADJUSTMENT

DON'T LET THE DOOR *hit you* WHERE THE GOOD LORD *split you.*

WHEN SOMEONE SNUBS YOUR DEVILED EGG RECIPE

WHEN SOMEONE SNUBS YOUR DEVILED EGG RECIPE

IF BRAINS WERE LEATHER,

you wouldn't have enough to saddle a Junebug.

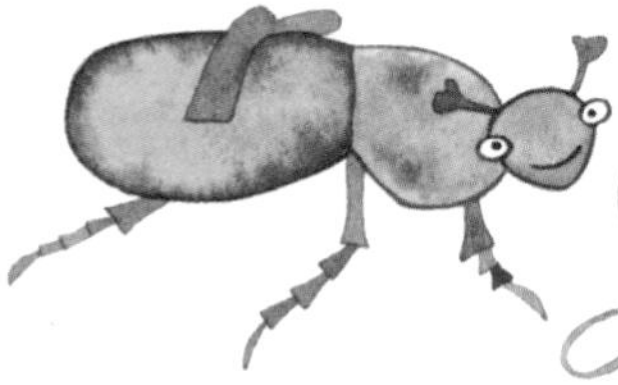

WHEN SOMEONE SNUBS YOUR DEVILED EGG RECIPE

HE AIN'T GOT THE *good sense God* GAVE A *goat.*

OR, EVEN WORSE, IF SOMEONE INSULTS YOUR MAMA'S CASSEROLE

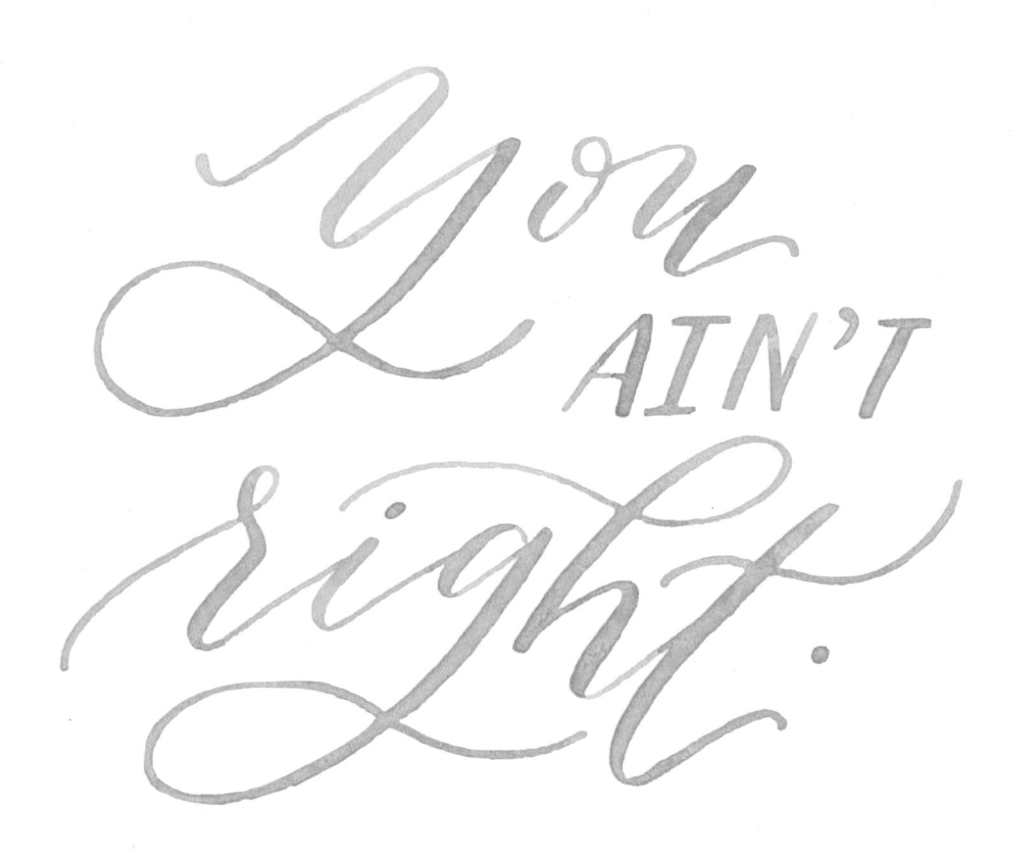

OR, EVEN WORSE, IF SOMEONE INSULTS YOUR MAMA'S CASSEROLE

OR, EVEN WORSE, IF SOMEONE INSULTS YOUR MAMA'S CASSEROLE

ACT LIKE YOU'VE *been to town before.*

WHEN SOMEONE CALLS DRESSING "STUFFING."

HE'S AS happy AS A dead pig IN THE sunshine.

WHEN SOMEONE SAYS "YOUSE GUYS" INSTEAD OF "Y'ALL"

Her cornbread AIN'T DONE in the middle.

WHEN YOU OVERHEAR SOMEBODY SAY UNSWEET TEA IS BETTER

We all have sick days, but here's how to translate them down South

HE'S BEEN FEELIN' *sick as a dawg.*

WHEN POLLEN IS EVERYWHERE — ON YOUR CAR, HOME, AND, WORST OF ALL, ALL UP IN YOUR ALLERGIES

I'm feelin' poorly today.

WHEN POLLEN IS EVERYWHERE — ON YOUR CAR, HOME, AND, WORST OF ALL, ALL UP IN YOUR ALLERGIES

WHEN POLLEN IS EVERYWHERE — ON YOUR CAR, HOME, AND, WORST OF ALL, ALL UP IN YOUR ALLERGIES

She's FEELING peckish.

WHEN POLLEN IS EVERYWHERE — ON YOUR CAR, HOME, AND, WORST OF ALL, ALL UP-IN YOUR ALLERGIES

HE'S BEEN

all laid up:

WHEN POLLEN IS EVERYWHERE — ON YOUR CAR, HOME, AND, WORST OF ALL, ALL UP IN YOUR ALLERGIES

I'M FEELIN' *under* THE *weather.*

WHEN POLLEN IS EVERYWHERE — ON YOUR CAR, HOME, AND, WORST OF ALL, ALL UP IN YOUR ALLERGIES

She's been stove up.

WHEN YOU'RE SICK DURING OUR ONE MONTH OF WINTER

I GOT THE *vapours.*

WHEN YOU'RE SICK DURING OUR ONE MONTH OF WINTER

I'M *fair* TO *middlin'*

WHEN YOU'RE SICK DURING OUR ONE MONTH OF WINTER

FOR THOSE DAYS THE HUMIDITY KNOCKS YOU RIGHT OUT

Maw Maw HAS BASICALLY BEEN AT death's door.

Paw Paw's
GOING
downhill
fast.

THESE ARE FOR WHEN THINGS GET REALLY BAD, Y'ALL

I'D HAVE TO
feel better
TO DIE.

He's playin' possum again.

WHEN YOUR CO-WORKER CALLS IN SICK TO WATCH THE BRAVES

If I felt
any better,
I'D DROP MY HARP
PLUMB THROUGH
THE CLOUD.

Talkin' about money definitely isn't taboo down South

WE WERE LIVIN' high on the hog.

HOW YOU FEEL WHEN YOUR TOMATO PLANTS START GROWING

I'M SO *poor* I COULDN'T JUMP OVER A *nickel* TO SAVE A *dime.*

THINGS YOU CAN SAY AFTER PAYING YOUR ELECTRICITY BILL IN THE SUMMERTIME

THINGS YOU CAN SAY AFTER PAYING YOUR ELECTRICITY BILL IN THE SUMMERTIME

He was so poor,

HE HAD A TUMBLEWEED AS A PET.

HE'D HAVE TO
borrow money
TO BUY
water to
cry with:

HOW TEXAN PARENTS FEEL AFTER THEY BUY THEIR KIDS' HOMECOMING MUMS

IF A TRIP AROUND
THE WORLD
COST A DOLLAR,

*I couldn't
get to the
state line.*

HOW TEXAN PARENTS FEEL AFTER THEY BUY THEIR KIDS' HOMECOMING MUMS

THEY DON'T HAVE A *pot to piss in.*

HOW TEXAN PARENTS FEEL AFTER THEY BUY THEIR KIDS' HOMECOMING MUMS

HE WAS AS *poor* AS *Job's turkey.*

HOW TEXAN PARENTS FEEL AFTER THEY BUY THEIR KIDS' HOMECOMING MUMS

You didn't think you'd get through this book without a food chapter, did you?

I'M SO
hungry
I COULD EAT
THE
north end
OF A
southbound
goat.

FOR THOSE MOMENTS YOU THINK YOU COULD ACTUALLY EAT BROOKLYN BARBECUE

I'm so full I'm about to pop.

WHAT TO TELL GRANNY WHEN SHE TRIES TO PUT MORE FOOD ON YOUR PLATE

WHAT TO TELL GRANNY WHEN SHE TRIES TO PUT MORE FOOD ON YOUR PLATE

I'm so full

I'M JUST MISERABLE.

WHAT TO TELL GRANNY WHEN SHE TRIES TO PUT MORE FOOD ON YOUR PLATE

I'm having a hankerin'.

WHEN ALL YOU REALLY WANT IS SOME FRIED CHICKEN

HE'S DRUNK AS *Cooter Brown.*

WHEN YOUR UNCLE DRINKS A LITTLE TOO MUCH AT THANKSGIVING

He's got a pickled liver.

WHEN YOUR UNCLE DRINKS A LITTLE TOO MUCH AT THANKSGIVING

MY EYES WERE

bigger

THAN MY

stomach.

WHEN YOU ORDER A MEAT, THREE VEGGIES AND DESSERT

And here's what you need to know for every other occasion life throws your way (like instant grits)

WHEN YOU ENCOUNTER SOMETHING PRETTY USELESS — LIKE UNSWEET TEA, OR SALAD AT A TAILGATE

IT DOESN'T *amount* TO A *hill* OF *beans.*

WHEN YOU ENCOUNTER SOMETHING PRETTY USELESS — LIKE UNSWEET TEA, OR SALAD AT A TAILGATE

You're just preaching to the choir.

WHEN SOMEONE SAYS THE SOUTH HAS THE BEST BARBECUE

I haven't seen you in a month of Sundays.

I AIN'T SEEN YOU SINCE YOU WERE *knee-high* TO A *grasshopper.*

What IN tarnation?

FOR THOSE MOMENTS YOU WANT TO CURSE BUT YOUR GRANNY IS NEARBY

WHAT IN THE *Sam Hill!*

FOR THOSE MOMENTS YOU WANT TO CURSE BUT YOUR GRANNY IS NEARBY

IT'S AS *scarce* AS *hen's teeth.*

WHEN YOU'RE LOOKING FOR GOOD GRITS OUTSIDE THE SOUTH

AND OF COURSE, FOR US PROCRASTINATORS *(But hey, we made it to the end of the book)*